Under the Shadow of the Almighty

Under the Shadow of the Almighty

by

Herbert Kiesler

This book is dedicated to my beloved wife Minodora.

Author: Dr. Herbert Kiesler
herbkiesler@gmail.com

Editor: Rupert Ham-Ying - tsatsui@gmail.com

Typesetting and Proofreading: Janice Schmidt
premiumadventistediting@gmail.com

Proofreading: Minodora Grigorean Kiesler, Basanthi Thavamani

Cover design: Cristy Castrejon, Graphic Designer, Oklahoma Academy
cristycastrejon@oklahomaacademy.org

This book was refined with the assistance of Gemini (AI) for editing and structure.

Unless otherwise indicated, all Scripture quotations are taken from the King James Version (KJV).

First published by Amazon on February 20, 2026

Printed in the USA by Barnes Printing | 2,000 Copies

barnesprinting.com

Table of Contents

Preface

After I retired, my wife and I began attending the University Church in Berrien Springs, Michigan, where several members approached us, curious to know who we were and to learn more about our background. As I shared pieces of my journey—including the hardships of the Great Depression and the terrors of living through city bombardments—those who listened were moved. They insisted that I put my story into writing. One woman even told me, "I'll be the first one to buy the book." While I didn't begin writing immediately, their encouragement planted a seed. Eventually, I sat down to record my eyewitness accounts, and this book is the result.

The second, and perhaps the most vital, purpose of this book is to address the universal struggle with fear. Throughout my life, I have faced seasons of profound terror. I think specifically of World War II, when my mother, our neighbors, and I looked death in the face. It is impossible to remain naturally calm when bombs are exploding around you and the sheer force of the air pressure knocks you to the ground. In those moments, I had to ask: "How can we overcome human fear when the impossible happens?"

I often recall the stories my father recounted to me from the Old Testament—stories of Moses and of Daniel in the lions' den. Daniel faced a deadly situation, yet he remained firm. He placed his faith in the Almighty God and found refuge there.

Through my own trials, I reached a turning point where I decided: "When I am in deep fear, I will look to the Almighty and make Him my refuge and strength."

My recommendation to you, my dear reader, is this: Read God's Word and let Him direct your ways. He is the Almighty; He can carry you through everything that frightens you. Whether you are facing sickness, the threat of deportation, or any other overwhelming trial, let Him guide your life.

The stories in this book are evidence of God guiding my wife and me in ways that, humanly speaking, seem unbelievable. My faith in God through Jesus Christ has become my foundation. I encourage you to turn to Him to overcome the fears that beset you. In every situation, He will help you. This has been my lived experience, and I promise you this: He will never let you down, and He will never disappoint you.

— Dr. Herbert Kiesler

Chapter 1

A Birth Amidst the Storm

May 17, 1931, was a beautiful, sunny Sunday morning in Dortmund, Germany. In stark contrast to the growing national turmoil and conflict, there was profound joy in the Kiesler home; a baby boy had been born to August and Martha Kiesler.

At that time, the country was desperately seeking new leadership. Paul von Hindenburg was the leader of the German nation, and he eventually appointed Adolf Hitler as Chancellor. This set the stage for Hitler to become the leader of the Third Reich. He was originally an Austrian citizen, but his background was framed in a way that made him appear to be a promising leader for the German people.

During World War I, Hitler had served as a messenger, carrying correspondence between the front lines. He lacked formal academic training; his only recognized talent was as an artist. Years earlier, he had applied to an art school in Vienna but was rejected. Following that failure, he spent much of his time in libraries, likely immersing himself in political ideologies, as he aspired to reach the highest levels of power.

The moment Hitler seized control of Germany, his true character was revealed. He began to rule with an iron fist. A strict system of censorship was established, ensuring that no publication reached the public without government approval. He sought total control over information, ruthlessly silencing any political arguments that might rise against him.

It is astounding that within only six years, Adolf Hitler managed to build a complete military machine, comprising a Navy, an Air Force, and an infantry equipped with sophisticated tank divisions. The latter was commanded by General Heinz Guderian, the architect of fast-moving armored warfare.

By 1939, Hitler was prepared to move forward with his plans for war. His first objectives were the invasions of Poland and then France. Amidst this mobilization, my father was conscripted. He had no choice but to obey orders. One morning, a sharp knock sounded at our door. There stood a military officer, presenting a government ordinance. He informed my father that he was to report to a specific office in town immediately—and he was told to bring an empty suitcase along with him.

When my father finally returned home later that day, he was in full uniform. The sight brought a stark realization: my father was no longer available to us; he now belonged to the government. The weeks and months that followed weighed heavily on my mother and me as we faced a future without him.

Hitler's Campaign Against the Jewish People

As Adolf Hitler made his final preparations for World War II, he simultaneously launched a campaign to eliminate all Jewish people from Germany. At the time, several of the neighbors in our apartment building were Jewish. Among them was the Katz family, who had two sons named Boobie and Heinz. Mr. Katz often came to our door and asked my father to light their stove so they could cook on the Sabbath. My father was always happy to help. Because the Katz family knew we also kept the Sabbath as a special day of worship, a genuine friendship formed between our families.

That friendship was soon overshadowed by a government decree: every Jewish person was required to wear a visible symbol of their identity. They were forced to wear a large yellow Star of David with the word "Jude" (Jew) printed in the center. It had to be displayed prominently on a lapel or the upper right of a garment. I can only imagine the humiliation and fear they felt walking down the street or riding the streetcar. Some tried to hide the star by holding a map over it, desperate to avoid the stares of others.

This atmosphere of dread culminated in what felt like the start of the Holocaust. Hitler ordered the mass incarceration of the Jewish population, and the Katz family was not spared.

Early one morning, while it was still dark and I was in bed, their older son, Boobie, knocked on our door. I heard him ask my mother, "Mrs. Kiesler, can you give me some water?" Surprised, my mother replied, "Boobie, surely you have water in your home." He answered quietly, "We must leave in twenty minutes." Hearing those words, even as a child, I realized with a heavy heart that they were being taken away, and we would never see them again. I felt a profound sadness for the plight of our friends.

Later that morning, as I got ready for school, I passed the Katz's apartment. A "Red Eagle" seal had been placed over the keyhole, a grim warning that anyone entering would face a severe penalty. When I reached the main business street, destruction was everywhere. The streetcars were running as usual, but the storefronts were unrecognizable. The thick glass windows of Jewish-owned shoe stores and clothing shops had been smashed, and the merchandise inside had been set on fire. The synagogue, which I had walked past many times, was completely vandalized.

As a Christian, I found this behavior intolerable. People were being condemned to death simply because of their religious convictions. Thousands were deported by bus and train. We later learned from eyewitnesses of the horrors in Poland: Jewish people were forced to dig their own mass graves, stand at the edge, and face machine-gun fire. Their bodies toppled into the very trench they had been forced to dig.

Hitler's Attack on Dissenters: The Courage of Dietrich Bonhoeffer

During this dark era, many Protestant theologians and pastors tried to align with Nazi ideology by "streamlining" their services. However, one man stood out as a beacon of resistance: Dietrich Bonhoeffer, perhaps the most brilliant of the Lutheran theologians.

A student of the renowned Adolf von Harnack, Dietrich Bonhoeffer certainly was acquainted with the critical approach to the Bible, yet he clung steadfastly to the literal teachings of Jesus. He was one of the few who dared to stand openly against the Nazi regime. Bonhoeffer maintained vital connections abroad, including with the Swiss theologian Karl Barth and the Bishop of Chichester in England. These relationships were a lifeline in his resistance work.

The danger hit home when Bonhoeffer learned that his brother-in-law, a Jewish lawyer who had worked for the German government, was to be summoned to a Nazi court the following day. Recognizing the immediate threat, Bonhoeffer rushed a message to him, urging him to flee with his family at once.

They drove through the night toward the Swiss border, a journey fraught with peril. When they arrived, they initially found it difficult to gain entry. However,

Bonhoeffer used his international connections to make arrangements, and the Swiss authorities eventually opened the border, allowing his sister, her husband, and their children to escape to safety. Meanwhile, the Gestapo—the German secret police—began tracking Bonhoeffer's every move, desperate to uncover his secret network.

This nighttime drama was the beginning of a long and harrowing ordeal for Bonhoeffer. He was eventually arrested in Berlin and sent to a concentration camp in southern Germany. Even in captivity, he remained a beacon of light. He formed close bonds with fellow prisoners, including British Air Force pilots, and was often asked to lead worship services.

The end came with a cruelty difficult to fathom. One morning, as the sound of distant Allied gunfire signaled that liberation was near, an executioner entered his cell. "Get ready," he was told. "Your execution will take place in fifteen or twenty minutes." Eyewitnesses report Bonhoeffer spent those final moments on his knees in fervent prayer. He was then led away to his death.

The Allies arrived at the gates the very next day. The timing of his execution was nothing short of satanic in its cruelty. Yet, in his life and in his final moments, Dietrich Bonhoeffer demonstrated the true meaning of being a Christian. He was willing to sacrifice everything for his faith and the truth. Through his sacrifice, he has left an unforgettable legacy for the rest of the world.

Then said Jesus
unto His disciples,
If any man will
come after Me,
let him deny
himself, and take
up his cross,
and follow Me.

—Matthew 16:24

Chapter 2

My Father's Influence

From the moment my father was conscripted into the German military, I was forced to navigate challenges far beyond my years. By the age of eight, I was already carrying responsibilities that most children never know. However, 1942 proved to be the most difficult year of my entire life.

I vividly remember one particular Sabbath morning that February. The air was biting cold as we dressed for church. Despite the festive feel of my mother being "beautifully dressed," a cloud hung over us. I mentioned to her that we had not heard from my father in some time.

"I know," she replied softly. "I understand he is in Russia now, and they are enduring a terrible winter."

Just as she spoke of the heavy snowfall, I spotted the mail carrier approaching our building. Seeing a letter in his hand, I dashed out to meet him, grabbed the envelope, and raced back to my mother.

"Oh," she said, her eyes lighting up. "A letter from Dad." But as she looked closer at the envelope, her voice faltered. "Son, this is not his handwriting."

She opened the letter and began to read. Within seconds, her face transformed into a mask of profound sadness. I peeked over her elbow, my eleven-year-old eyes scanning the page. The words are burned into my memory: "Dear Mrs. Kiesler, I am very sorry to let you know that your husband did not return to his unit. No personal belongings were found."

The message was clear: my father was gone.

In a state of shock, I pivoted and bolted from the apartment. I ran blindly into the street, circling block after block in a desperate, aimless hunt for some kind of escape. It was a long time before I came back to my senses and returned home. I could not reconcile the reality of that letter with the man I knew. My father was my best friend and my most trusted advisor; he was the one who guided my education and shaped my character. Now, he was gone forever.

I found myself asking a question that would haunt me for years: "Who do I have now?" My mother was wonderful—the loveliest person I could have asked for—but there were certain struggles she couldn't fully navigate with me. As a young boy trying to hold onto my faith in Christ and follow His divine guidance amid such incredible, terrifying times, the void of my father's absence felt unbearable.

My father was always deeply interested in faith. Every night, he would call me to him, and I would sit on his lap as he told me the classic stories of the Old Testament—stories of Moses, Joshua, Daniel, and many others. Years later, a university professor I had remarked, "Parents who do not teach their children these classical stories are unwise." He was right; the world would look very different today if more children were raised with a strong biblical foundation.

Following my father's death in 1942, my childhood changed irrevocably. Living without him by my side was a heavy burden. He had always been invested in my future, often expressing his great desire that I would become a missionary and travel to foreign lands to share the story of Jesus. While life eventually took a different turn, his spiritual influence remained the bedrock of my character.

For He shall
give His angels
charge over thee,
to keep thee
in all thy ways.

—Psalm 91:11

Chapter 3

Miracles Amidst Ruin

A brief moment of normalcy occurred when I attended an exhibition of Russian wooden model homes at the Westfalenhallen in Dortmund—the world's largest wooden structure at the time. Shortly after, however, I contracted scarlet fever and was hospitalized in isolation for two weeks. When I finally returned home, my mother had prepared my bed with such care; it was heartwarming and comforting to slide into those clean, fresh sheets. I remember saying, "Oh Mom, it's so good to be home."

But even then, a quiet voice in my mind asked: *How long can this peace last?*

The answer came soon. I still remember the night when the sirens wailed from the rooftops. All lights were extinguished. Terrified of moving in the pitch blackness, I scrambled to dress as my mother and I rushed toward the basement for shelter. When I reached the main floor, I glanced out the window at the neighboring lot and looked straight into the heart of an exploding bomb.

The sheer force of the air pressure knocked me off my feet, sending me tumbling down the stairs. I collided with a woman and her baby carriage, and we all landed in a heap at the bottom of the basement stairs. The air was thick with suffocating smoke. Fortunately, provision had been made for such a moment: a "breakthrough" hole in the wall, filled with loose bricks, led to an adjacent apartment block. We pushed through and escaped the smoke.

Standing on the sidewalk across the street, I watched while smoke poured through the roof of our four-story building. I turned to my mother and asked, "What is going to happen now?"

Our loss was put into an even sharper perspective when a church elder pedaled up on his bicycle. He brought grim news: "Have you heard? We have lost our faithful organist." It was horrifying to learn that she had been killed in the blast, her head found in the street gutter. We stood there on the street alone—no belongings, no home, and no father to protect us.

In those moments, I was grateful for my Christian upbringing. My father had always taught me that God was watching over us. He used to tell me a story from his own service experience in World War I: he was riding the lead horse of a six-horse team, pulling an artillery gun in France. Suddenly, shrapnel struck the lead horse. The explosion killed every other horse in the team, yet my father walked away without a single scratch.

Following the bombing, my mother and I were directed to the massive cellars of the Union Brewery, where the government had set up cots for displaced people. But sleep was impossible. Eventually, we were relocated to another house, but that beautiful home, too, was eventually destroyed.

Chapter 4

Separated From My Mother

Finally, in late 1942, the government enacted a plan to evacuate all children from the cities to the safer regions of Bavaria. I had to pack my suitcases and walk to the train station. There, with about a hundred other boys from my school, I boarded a train headed for the distant town of Prien.

Upon our arrival, we were guided to a former youth hostel that had been converted into a multifaceted school, which included classrooms, dormitories, and a cafeteria. This would be our home for the next year.

Our daily program was two-fold. In the morning, we attended standard academic classes. However, the afternoons were dedicated to the field. We were led by two young ex-soldiers who trained us as if we were a voluntary military youth corps. They placed a heavy emphasis on survival skills. We were taken into dense forests and through rugged mountain terrain, where they taught us how to orient ourselves so we could find our way back home.

Beyond our training, we were also tasked with supporting the local farming families, many of whom had seen their husbands and sons sent to the front lines. The farmers certainly took advantage of our labor. I vividly remember the grueling work of the potato harvest. Once the plow sliced through the soil, we scrambled to gather the potatoes into baskets, racing to finish before the team surged back around for the next pass. It was a relentless test of speed and endurance.

Our time in Prien was relatively short. Before long, we were relocated further into the heart of the region to the beautiful town of Nussdorf in Bavaria.

In Nussdorf, most of the prominent properties were owned by one influential man. With the government's backing, he had built a large, modern hotel featuring its own butcher shop and bakery. Despite these resources, the food prepared for us students was miserable. We were served meager, low-quality rations while the cupboards were clearly full.

Determined to uncover the truth, several boys crept to the kitchen windows after dark. What they saw was a betrayal. The teachers were feasting on first-class meats and exquisite sweets, enjoying a world of indulgence while we were left to grow hungrier by the day.

A few boys befriended the owner's adopted daughter, Lilly. In an act of kindness—or perhaps rebellion of her own—she provided them with a key to the sausage storage room and a supply of fresh buns. One night, the group slipped into the chamber, sat down in the dark, and finally helped themselves to a decent meal.

Unfortunately, the owner was outside that night. As a member of the Volkssturm (People's Guard), he was vigilant. Noticing a faint sliver of light escaping from the storage room window, he rushed inside to investigate. He flung open the door, standing with his legs spread to block the exit, and caught the boys mid-meal. Most of the group managed to dive past his legs and vanish into the night, but my friend Helmut was not so lucky.

Helmut, a tough and gifted athlete, finally returned to our quarters exhausted and bruised from a "licking" by the owner. When he collapsed into his bunk and I asked what had happened, he simply snapped, "Shut up!" I knew better than to ask again and went back to sleep.

The next morning, the classroom was in an uproar. The teachers had been notified of the "theft" and were furious. They informed the boys that they had violated the law and would be sent to a Nazi correction center—a threat the Party took very seriously. However, the boys did not back down.

"We may have to go to a correction center," they challenged the teachers, "but what about you? Every night you sit there feasting while we are fed garbage."

The room fell deathly silent. Realizing their own hypocrisy had been exposed and could be reported, the staff dropped the charges immediately. The threat of the correction center vanished, and the case was closed.

The End of the War

I was still attending school in Nussdorf when the day we would never forget finally arrived. The war was over; Germany had lost. In the early spring of 1945, the distant, rhythmic rumbling of the first approaching French Allied forces became louder each day. We were still staying at the Schneiderhof when the first signs of the occupation appeared.

A single Jeep carrying four American soldiers drove into town. They flew a white flag—a clear signal that they intended to negotiate with the mayor. Fortunately, our mayor was a man of reason. He understood that any attempt to defend the town would be futile; he knew that within five minutes, the Allied Air Force could flatten our beautiful streets and leave nothing but debris. "No," he declared, "there will be no defense here."

Soon after, the main Army arrived. A column of Sherman tanks rolled through, looking so pristine that they appeared as if they had never seen combat. They were passing through on their way toward Italy.

Following the tanks, the rest of the American infantry moved in to occupy the town.

Before the tanks arrived, I witnessed an incident that remains vivid in my mind. A young, unarmed German serviceman in uniform raised his arms in surrender. An American soldier approached him, but instead of hostility, he offered a gesture of humanity: he handed the German a bottle of liquor. The German took a sip, handed it back to the GI, and for a brief moment, they were just two men rather than enemies.

Moments after this, a highly decorated German officer stepped out of a building across the street. To the utter shock of the American troops, he began to speak to them in perfect, fluent American English. A crowd of soldiers and officers gathered around him, stunned. He then told his story: he had been living in America and had only returned to Germany on vacation to visit relatives when the war broke out. Trapped by the borders, the German government drafted him, forcing him into military service.

As the American army settled in, they began requisitioning private residences, converting several homes into their official headquarters. The long, dark chapter of the war was finally closing, and a new, uncertain era was beginning.

Two particular incidents from the early days of the occupation remain etched in my memory. One day, a friend and I were walking past a field kitchen when we noticed a short, jolly cook singing a popular tune: "She drives the limousine and I buy the gasoline." He had a towering pile of freshly baked pancakes resting on top of a large sugar bag.

He looked up and asked us if we were hungry. "Of course," we replied. "Take these and get going," he said with a smile. It was a simple, incredibly kind gesture that meant the world to two hungry boys.

On another occasion, I was walking by the gates when I met a young sergeant from an American artillery unit. We struck up a conversation, and he invited me into the room that he shared with another soldier—a Spanish-speaking man from Los Angeles. The sergeant had just received a care package from his parents in the United States. He picked up an item and asked, "Have you ever tried this? You must try it." His generosity was the beginning of a genuine friendship.

Once he told me, "On Sunday, I don't have to be in uniform. I can dress as a civilian, and if you wouldn't mind, I'd like to hike into the mountains with you." I told him I would be delighted. We spent that Sunday morning hiking through the beautiful Bavarian landscape. Upon returning to his quarters, he opened another parcel from home filled with treats and let me try everything inside.

Eventually, his unit was ordered to move out, but before he left, he took down my home address. A year later, a letter from Lincoln, Nebraska, arrived for me. Donald F. Copes was home.

In his letter, he wrote, "I know you guys need a lot of things. My wife, Mary, works as a secretary in a department store and is earning good money. Tell me what you need, and I will send it." Though there was much we lacked, I didn't want to ask for too much. I requested only two bars of soap, which were impossible to find, and a small package of cocoa powder to mix with our milk. Soon after, a parcel arrived containing two large bars of soap and a tin of Hershey's cocoa.

I maintained contact with Donald for a long time, deeply moved by his character. Years later, while I was studying at the seminary at Andrews University in Michigan, I met a summer school teacher from Lincoln, Nebraska. I asked him if he could look up Donald F. Copes upon his return. He eventually wrote back to tell me that he had located the family; Donald was now operating a gas station in West Covina, California. I reached out to him there, but sadly, I never received another response.

Despite the silence, those encounters shaped my worldview. I never harbored hostile feelings toward people of other nations or races because I saw firsthand the kindness that can exist between supposed enemies.

Thy word is
a lamp unto
my feet, and
a light unto
my path.

—*Psalm 119:105*

Chapter 5

The Long Road Home

When the war ended, we students in Nussdorf were suddenly left without supervision. With no public transportation running to the north, some of us decided to pack our backpacks and hit the road on foot, even though we knew the journey home could take weeks.

Then, we received a stroke of luck: a military truck, which had been requisitioned by a local business, was headed for Munich. We climbed on. Along the way, as the other passengers disembarked at their destinations, some kindly gave us a bit of money. We stayed with the truck until we reached the Danube River.

By 9 PM that evening, Erwin Birkner and I were walking through a small town when a woman called out to us from a window. "Boys, there is a curfew! You cannot stay in the street." She invited us inside and took us under her wing. After a light supper, she showed us to a garden house with a comfortable mattress and a barrel of rainwater for washing. The next morning, she fed us breakfast before we set off again. I remember that shortly after hitting the road, I decided my heavy blanket was too much to carry and tossed it into a ditch—a true sign of my determination to move fast.

We pushed on for another thirteen kilometers. Exhausted, we finally stopped at a small farmhouse and asked the woman there if we could stay the night. She had just finished milking her cows and welcomed us in without hesitation. Moments later, she placed a feast before us: a large German pancake for each of us, a bowl filled with smoked sausages, and fresh glasses of milk.

"Go upstairs," she told us once we were full. "There is a bed wide enough for both of you." We slept deeply. After another wonderful breakfast the following morning, we said our goodbyes to those lovely people. Our journey continued like this—moving from town to town and village to village—relying entirely on the map and the mercy of strangers.

One of the most intense experiences of our journey was the ride we secured on a long oil tanker train. We found seats on a small platform directly behind the locomotive. As the train gathered speed, we felt a sense of progress, but that quickly turned to peril when we entered a long tunnel.

Inside the dark tunnel, the engineer began stoking the locomotive's fire. Thick smoke and glowing, fiery sparks were blown directly over us. In a desperate attempt to protect myself, I pulled out my brand-new winter coat and huddled underneath it. By the time we emerged into the light and arrived in Schweinfurt, my coat was ruined—riddled with holes from the glowing embers. I had no choice but to throw it away.

When we arrived, the authorities ordered all the returning German soldiers to disembark and line up on the station platform. We teenagers were not permitted to reboard the train; instead, American personnel escorted us to the mayor's office for registration. From there, we were sent to a nearby school that had been converted into a temporary shelter.

No food was provided. To survive, we were sent out to abandoned gardens to scavenge for old potatoes that had been left in the ground from previous seasons. We dug them up, gathered what we could, and carried them back to the school to boil them. It was meager sustenance, but it was all we had.

One day, Erwin and I ventured into the city of Schweinfurt. The open marketplace was nearly empty, but we managed to find a few carrots to chew on. As we walked, an elderly lady following behind us asked, "You boys, are you hungry?"

"Yes, we are," we replied honestly.

She invited us to her home, a small apartment on the upper floor of a modest house where she lived with her daughter. They shared what they had: a simple meal of boiled potatoes and green lettuce. We were deeply grateful. On another day, we found an open restaurant serving the same simple food. When we finished and asked for the bill, the staff told us not to worry—the meal had already been paid for by another patron.

Finally, after days of scavenging and small kindnesses, we were able to board a train headed for Frankfurt.

We arrived at the Frankfurt train station to find it completely destroyed. With the curfew approaching, we found ourselves stranded once more. Suddenly, my companion spotted a Red Cross nurse. She kindly invited us to come to her mother's apartment, where we were treated with extraordinary warmth. The daughter brought us food from the hospital where she worked. The mother offered us an extra bedroom to rest in until we were ready to attempt the final leg of our journey. Finally, we both reached Erwin's home, where I stayed overnight. The next morning, I continued my journey to Dorstfeld. There, I went to the home of my uncle, Albert Mauritz, and stayed with him for a couple of days.

My next destination was my birthplace, Dortmund. However, I still had to reach the village of Kleinenwieden, where my mother had relocated after our home in Dortmund was destroyed. I walked another 100 kilometers, arriving on the verge of total collapse. Yet the sheer joy of our reunion infused me with a sudden, renewed energy.

Starting Over

Life on the farm was a new beginning. I became well-acquainted with the animals, specifically the six cows I was tasked with tending. It was a constant battle of wills; I tried to keep them on their small patch of grass while they stubbornly lunged for the neighboring wheat field. I did this for several weeks, but at fourteen years old, I knew I needed to find profitable work. We had no source of income—the government had collapsed, and my mother's pension had vanished.

With my formal schooling cut off, I sought the best occupation available. I found work at a furniture factory in Hessisch Oldendorf, ten kilometers away. I commuted by train every day. Eventually, I signed a three-year contract to apprentice as a cabinet maker. Upon earning my diploma, I was qualified for more complex work and higher pay.

As things improved, I considered buying a beautiful BMW motorcycle, but a deeper ambition prevailed. I chose instead to invest my earnings in an interior architecture school. It was a highly rated institution with a rigorous discipline that I grew to love. I thrived on the intensive program, especially the challenges of design and complex calculations.

However, a question of conscience began to weigh on me. As I looked toward a career in architecture, I realized I would struggle to honor the Sabbath and keep the fourth commandment. Following my heart, I decided to enroll in the Adventist seminary.

I set aside my drawing supplies and committed myself to the Marienhöhe Seminary in Darmstadt.

The Colporteur: Selling Books in Germany

To support my education, I found myself with few options. Finding short-term employment in post-war Germany was a difficult task, so I finally decided to sell Christian books as a "colporteur." This commitment required me to spend the entire break between school years going door-to-door—a prospect I had always dreaded.

Initially, I was far from enthusiastic. I told myself, "I am not meant to be a salesman." I had just completed my studies in interior design at a highly reputable private school; the idea of knocking on doors felt beneath my training. However, the Lord opened a path for me, and it turned out to be one of the most transformative experiences of my life.

My routine was rigorous. At each visit, I had to make a professional introduction, give a demonstration of the literature, explain my purpose, and discuss the prices. By the grace of God, I was remarkably successful. In just one summer, I earned enough money to cover my tuition and living expenses for the entire upcoming school year.

When the time came to return to the seminary, the books needed to be delivered. My mother stepped in to help with the distribution. She later told me, "If you had stayed home, there were seventeen families who had asked for you to come back and study the Bible with them." This was a profound realization for me. It was encouraging to know that the books I sold were not just merchandise; they were opening hearts to the Word of God.

Chapter 6

To Sweden by Faith

The following summer, my roommate, Wilfried—who had spent the previous year selling religious books in Sweden—approached me with a suggestion. He had been very successful there and proposed that I join him.

"That isn't so easy for me," I replied. "I don't know the language, and I don't have a motorcycle or a car."

He was completely undeterred. "You can ride with me," he said. "I have a heavy-duty, two-seater motor scooter. Here, take my Swedish grammar book and study it; you'll be prepared by the time we arrive."

He clearly had a high opinion of my linguistic abilities. The reality, however, was quite different. When I opened that grammar book and looked at the Swedish text, I could make neither head nor tail of it.

Finally, Wilfried and I set out from the seminary. I settled in as "co-pilot" on his rugged motor scooter, our few possessions strapped down for the long trek north. Our route took us across the heart of Germany and through the windswept plains of Denmark. After crossing two stretches of sea, we reached Malmö. There, we were met with an immediate challenge: navigating Sweden's road system, where traffic flowed unexpectedly on the left.

We pushed on until exhaustion finally overcame Wilfried. "I'm too tired to continue," he admitted. "I need you to take over." In hindsight, it was a reckless decision; we were both drained. I managed to keep us on the road until we hit a sharp curve to the right. As I leaned into the turn, Wilfried—who had fallen fast asleep behind me—remained upright and stiff. His dead weight threw us off balance, and we careened into a deep ditch.

As I lay pinned under the scooter, I realized that the windshield had cut into my forehead. I was fortunate that it had a rubberized edge, which likely prevented a far worse injury. With my coat stained with blood, I lay helplessly in the ditch until a dramatic sight appeared above: a Volvo taxi had pulled over at the scene. Two men scrambled down the embankment, lifted me off the scooter, and carried me to the car.

I was rushed to a hospital fourteen kilometers away. It was a Friday afternoon, and as the doctors took scans of my head, I felt a wave of anxiety wash over me. Here I was, far from home in a Swedish hospital bed, wondering how I would ever pay the bills.

However, on the Sabbath, I received a wonderful surprise. Three men entered my room; one carried Adventist literature to distribute to the patients, while another brought a brown bag overflowing with delicious fruit. They told me that a group from the local Adventist church had held a special prayer meeting for me the night before. I also discovered that the woman who had witnessed our accident was the one who had called and paid for the taxi.

The doctors kept me until Monday to ensure I was stable. During that time, Wilfried was invited to stay in the home of a sea captain's widow. This entire experience was a profound lesson in the importance of trusting the Lord.

On Monday, Wilfried picked me up, and we found lodging in the home of a retired church member. Our host had lived in the United States for forty years, where he had once owned a fleet of ships. After resting there for several days, we finally set out for Ekebyholm College in Rimbo, Sweden. When we arrived, however, the college pastor greeted me with a look of pure skepticism.

"What are you planning to do here in Sweden?" he asked. I told him I intended to sell books. He laughed. "How can you sell books when you don't even know the language?"

I didn't answer him—mostly because I didn't understand a word he said.

On the following Monday, we traveled another 400 kilometers to reach Eksharad, Sweden where Wilfried had worked the previous year. There, I was introduced to an elderly woman named Agda, the owner of a beautiful estate complete with a small pond. When Wilfried told her about our accident and mentioned that I was still suffering from a broken collar-bone, she immediately offered to pay for a clinic visit. Instead, we consulted a local physician about forty miles away. His advice was simple but daunting: "Keep your arm in a sling and be careful when you ride your bicycle."

Agda's home became our sanctuary; it was the place we returned to every weekend. She was an incredibly generous soul, providing us with meals that were beyond our imagination.

To begin our work, Wilfried took me to a large home in a town called Höje. The owner, Petrus Westlund, was an elderly man of deep faith. His home was filled with diplomas from various biblical courses he had completed, and he told me that seven evangelists had stayed there before me. He graciously invited me to stay as long as I needed, giving me a large living room equipped with a beautiful couch and a home organ.

The next challenge was mobility. I had no car and no motorcycle. Realizing my predicament, Petrus said, "My sons are in the painting business now and no longer need their bicycles. There are two nearly new ones in the shed; go in, pick the one you like, and take it." I used that bicycle from the beginning to the end of my time in Sweden. Remarkably, I never once had a flat tire.

Adhering to the doctor's instructions was a challenge. My healing collarbone required a sling, leaving me to navigate the bike one-handed while balancing a heavy illustration album in the handlebar basket. It was a precarious way to travel from home to home, but I pressed on.

Communication remained my greatest hurdle. Wilfried had helped me memorize a brief, phonetic introduction in Swedish, but that was all I had. I still remember approaching a gentleman sitting on his front steps where he was repairing fishing nets. When I delivered my rehearsed lines in my halting Swedish, a wide smile spread across his face. For a long time, I had to stumble through conversations, but then one day, it simply "clicked." The barrier vanished, and I found I had become competent in the Swedish language.

The first day I set out to sell books in Höje, I returned to Petrus' home discouraged. When he asked how my business had gone, I had to admit I had found no success.

Petrus didn't let me dwell on it. "Try again tomorrow," he said simply.

The next evening, I returned with a different story; it had been a day of great success. Petrus was overjoyed. I suspect he had spent the day calling all his relatives in town, urging them to buy a book from the young man staying in his home.

As the days passed, my confidence in God's guidance grew. I began each morning with an early start, determined to follow wherever the path led. Because I was working in remote rural areas where no hotels or motels existed, I relied entirely on the kindness of strangers. Every evening, as I reached the last house on my route, I would ask the residents if I could stay the night. Remarkably, I was never once turned down. My hosts always provided me with hearty food and a warm bed, and I remain deeply grateful for the incredible spirit of the Swedish people.

I remember one particularly special moment as I was pushing my bicycle through a thick layer of sand along a dusty country road under a scorching sun. I spotted a small house built atop a steep hill. Despite the heat, I pushed my bike up the incline and knocked on the door. A young lady opened it and invited me in.

As I explained the purpose of my visit, I heard her mother's voice calling from the bedroom. Though she was ill, she told her daughter, "Go ahead and buy that book." She handed over the money, and the sale was complete. Then, the young lady looked at me and asked, "Are you hungry?"

Since there were no stores along those winding country roads, I was indeed famished. "Yes, I am," I replied. She had just finished baking a cake that was as yellow as an egg yolk. She sliced it while it was still warm and served it to me with a large glass of cold, fresh milk. It was the best meal I could have imagined.

Before I left, she said, "I will play and sing a song for you." She sat down and performed a beautiful Christian hymn. As

I said goodbye and headed back down the hill, I felt a massive boost of energy—not just from the cake, but from the spirit of the encounter. It was a moment of grace I shall never forget.

A similar moment of grace occurred in a different district. I knocked on the door of a beautiful farmhouse, and the woman who answered invited me inside. "I am a nutritionist by profession," she told me, "and I would like to prepare a meal for you."

In no time, the table was laden with the most delicious and healthful food I had ever seen. During our conversation, she mentioned that her fiancé was a theology student at Uppsala University. Once supper was over, she led me to her piano. "Come and sing with me," she said. Together, we sang a beautiful hymn that asked the Lord to take her hands and lead her safely to her journey's end. It was another deeply meaningful experience that left me feeling elevated and spiritually renewed.

Further Education

Looking back on my time in Sweden, I am struck by the extraordinary friendliness and personal support of the people. While I was sad to leave such a kind nation, I knew I had to return to Germany to finish my studies.

After three years of intense study, I completed the program and was called to the ministry in Hamburg. I served there for a year and a half until a church leader encouraged me to pursue further studies at Emmanuel Missionary College (now

Andrews University) in Berrien Springs, Michigan. He believed a master's degree would broaden my perspective, and he promised, "When you come back home, I will be there to meet you at the port."

The journey to America was a leap of faith—one that would change the course of my life forever.

Chapter 7

Crossing the Atlantic Ocean

I traveled to the harbor to board my ship—a converted wheat freighter bound for New York City. Upon my arrival, I was immediately faced with the necessity of supporting myself in a new country. Soon I found work in a "sweatshop" to save for my tuition. There I crossed paths with a former schoolmate, Gerhard Hasel, who had recently purchased a used Dodge for $200.

We decided to drive from New York to Berrien Springs together and split the costs. We had no money for hotels, so we slept in the car. My friend suggested I take the front seat while he rolled himself in a blanket to sleep on the grass outside. It was a miserable, freezing night. In the morning, I peeked out the window and saw Gerhard Hasel, wrapped in his blanket, which was now covered in a layer of white frost. He stood up, shook off the ice, and jumped back into the car. We kept driving until we reached the college just in time for registration.

Registration took place in the old gymnasium, where teachers were lined up at tables. My first hurdle was to pass an English proficiency test. They handed me a thick booklet, and as I flipped through the pages, my heart sank. It had been years since I had taken an English class, and I felt completely unprepared.

Fortunately, a compassionate French teacher from Switzerland, Dr. Augsburger, sensed my distress. "Herbert," he said gently, "can you just write a small essay for me in English instead?" I sat down and poured my thoughts into a meaningful essay, then handed it back. He looked it over for a moment and then smiled. "You go ahead and register."

I initially signed up for sixteen credit hours, including a daunting course on philosophical biology. It proved to be too much for someone still coming to grips with the English language, so I eventually dropped it, settling on a fourteen-hour load. Despite the challenges, I thrived. Over the next two years, I compressed a four-year program into a focused period of study, proudly graduating with my Bachelor of Arts degree in the spring of 1961.

Canadian Interlude

After completing my first year at Emmanuel Missionary College, I decided to spend the summer selling books in Canada to earn money for my second year. Several fellow students had found great success there and encouraged me to follow their lead. I contacted the publishing director in Oshawa, Ontario, who welcomed me to the field.

When I arrived in Oshawa, the first order of business was transportation. The director took me to a local car dealership, where the salesman happened to be a former student of my college. The director asked if there were any cars available for $200.

"I might have something," the salesman replied, leading us to an old Buick. As I sat down in the driver's seat, I realized something was missing. "How do you start this thing?" I asked.

"You just have to hold these two wires together," he said casually. "Otherwise, it runs fine." With no other options, I bought the car.

Because I didn't have a Canadian driver's license, I had to take a driving test in this standard stick-shift vehicle. After a quick lesson from the salesman, I went to the exam, but I made a small error while shifting gears. The officer told me to return in two weeks to try again.

As it turned out, I didn't need the car after all. The mission field I was assigned to was better suited for a bicycle. The director had me park the old Buick on the street by his house and leave it there. Some Jamaican schoolmates, who were also canvassing, eventually bought the car from me. When I ran into them later at a camp meeting and asked how the Buick was faring, they laughed and said they had driven it for a few days before ending up in a ditch and leaving it there for good.

I continued my work on two wheels around Virgil, Ontario. One evening, when I knocked on a farmhouse door at 9:00 PM, an elderly lady opened it and immediately asked if she could give me something to eat. I couldn't answer; I simply pointed to my cheek, which was painfully swollen from a severe tooth infection.

"I see you have a problem," she said kindly. She turned to her husband, a gentle man resting in his armchair, and asked him to call the local clinic. They realized the situation was serious. Remarkably, the doctor and nurse were still at the office; after her husband explained my condition, the doctor told them to bring me in immediately. The elderly man loaded my bicycle into the trunk of his old Pontiac and drove me straight to the clinic.

The doctor and nurse worked for two hours, finally extracting the troublesome molar at 11:00 PM. They did a splendid job and charged me very little for the emergency surgery. When I walked back into the waiting room, I was moved to find the elderly man still sitting there, waiting to drive me home. I was profoundly touched by the selflessness of this couple, who I later learned were Mennonites.

My time in the Niagara Falls area was generally enjoyable, though it wasn't without drama. At one point, I was stopped by the police after someone falsely reported that I was distributing “communist literature.” I was taken to the police station for an investigation, but a local church officer came to my aid. Everything was quickly resolved in my favor, and I was allowed to continue my ministry.

By the end of the summer, I returned to the United States with enough money to cover the entire cost of my second school year. Once again, my needs had been met through hard work and the kindness of strangers.

The Road Back to Germany

In 1961, I graduated with a BA in Theology from Emmanuel Missionary College. I faced a significant hurdle. I had planned to marry Minodora Grigorean, a young lady in Germany, but because she was born in Romania, she faced a grueling five-year waiting period for a U.S. visa. The only solution was for me to return to Germany, marry her there, and then apply for her visa through the American Consulate. However, my funds were completely depleted. I found myself asking, "Now what?"

Then, a miracle happened. While I was walking down the hallway of the administration building at Emmanuel Missionary College, I crossed paths with Dr. Augsburger. He stopped me and asked, "I am taking a group of students to Collonges, France. Would you be interested in joining us?"

I was stunned and overjoyed. Furthermore, he further offered me $75 to teach conversational German to the students during the trip. In my eyes, this was God's direct answer to my prayer. From that moment onward, everything moved rapidly toward graduation. Receiving my hard-earned diploma was a moment of immense pride, but I didn't yet realize it was only the beginning—the impetus that would eventually lead me to my ultimate goal: a doctorate.

Following the graduation ceremony, while most students rushed home, I secured a ride to O'Hare Airport in Chicago. After paying $25 for my airfare and waiting three hours, I began the first leg of my journey. Eventually, I met up with my companions at a Greyhound station in New York, and we headed for the port to board our ship to France.

This voyage was far more lively than my first crossing, as the ship was filled with students. About a week into the journey, as we reached the English Channel, an oarsman invited one of us into the booth to take the ship's wheel. He stood by, watching as we guided the vessel toward Bordeaux in France.

Once we disembarked, I faced a different challenge. Because I was an invitee and not a regular student on the tour, my food and lodging were not covered. That first night in France, I had to sleep on the last seat of the tour bus. It was bitterly cold, but I was young and had grown accustomed to hardship. The next morning, a kind friend allowed me to use the shower in his hotel room, and I managed to find a good breakfast.

As Dr. Augsburger guided us through historical churches and the sites of ancient castles, I remained convinced that the Lord would provide. My faith was rewarded; whenever a meal or a bed was needed, a spot always seemed to open up—often because a student was missing or a space was canceled. I never went hungry. Our journey eventually concluded at the Collonges-sous-Salève Adventist College, nestled near the Swiss border.

From Geneva, our group began to disperse. Some students journeyed toward Bogenhofen, Austria, but my heart was set on Germany. Munich was my first destination, and upon arrival, I immediately sent a telegram to my sweetheart in Stuttgart to let her know I was nearing the end of my long trek.

I arrived in Stuttgart at midnight. The station was hushed, and as I stepped off the train onto the dark platform, the air was perfectly still. Only two weak lamps cast a dim, amber glow over the concrete. I peered into the shadows, searching the far end of the platform for any sign of my wife-to-be. There, in the distance, I detected a solitary figure waiting for me.

We began to walk toward one another. With every step we took, our silhouettes sharpened until no doubt remained: we had finally found each other. Then came that long-awaited, unforgettable moment—the warmth of a deep embrace and a kiss that bridged years of distance and uncertainty. With hearts overflowing, Minodora and I caught the very last streetcar of the evening. Bathed in its bright interior lights, we looked at one another face-to-face for the first time in four years. It was a moment of pure, overwhelming joy—the greatest blessing of our lives.

The following days were a whirlwind of joy and purpose. Together, we planned the most significant details of our future:

the date and the place we would finally celebrate our wedding.

Chapter 8

A New Life and a Shared Mission

Our wedding was both a solemn and a joyous occasion. We were honored to have Pastor R. Dettmar, president of the South German Union of Seventh-day Adventists, officiate. During the ceremony, he gave me a charge I have never forgotten: to remain a loyal husband through even the most difficult moments and to always cherish the bride standing beside me. I have held that promise in my heart for over sixty-four years. Following the service, our friends and relatives gathered at my mother-in-law's home in Dörrenbach, Saar, to celebrate our new life together.

However, our happiness was immediately tested. On the very night after our wedding, my wife fell gravely ill with a whooping cough. She had contracted it from a young nephew, who had unknowingly brought the illness to our celebration. This unexpected trial put our plans on hold as she underwent medical treatment. Once she recovered, we found short-term employment together, working until we had just enough funds to board a 10,000-ton United States liner bound for New York.

The winter crossing in January was treacherous. The waves were so violent that the ship couldn't even dock at its scheduled stop in southern England. Most passengers remained in their cabins, too seasick to eat, but we finally made it to the New York harbor. There we met my wife's cousin, Alma.

Fortunately, we met a young scientist on the ship who was associated with the aerospace engineer Wernher von Braun. When we mentioned that we needed to reach Michigan, he offered a generous solution. "I have my car parked at a farm in New Jersey," he told us. "I'm driving to Toledo, Ohio, and you are welcome to join me." My cousin, Alma, kindly drove us all to the farm in New Jersey to retrieve the car. From there, we traveled with him to Toledo, where we eventually caught a Greyhound bus for the final leg of our journey to Berrien Springs, Michigan.

We arrived in the teeth of a freezing Michigan winter with thirteen pieces of luggage, only to learn that the apartment reserved for us had been given to someone else. In that moment of desperation, a schoolmate appeared in a Volkswagen. Somehow, we managed to fit ourselves and our belongings into the small car, and he took us to a place to stay the night. By the next morning, we had found another apartment and were finally able to move in.

I returned to my studies in order to complete my MA in Systematic Theology. My path then led me into the heart of city evangelism, specifically in Detroit, Michigan. I will never forget the climax of that campaign. Pastor George Vandeman held a massive meeting at the Ford Auditorium, where he spoke on the sobering topic, "When No Man Can Buy or Sell." Seeing a crowd of 20,000 people and hearing the thunderous voices of the mass choirs was a life-changing experience. That summer, my wife and I visited countless homes, inviting people to the meetings.

Evangelism in the city was not without danger. I vividly remember ringing one doorbell only to have a man answer with a gun tucked under his arm; I backed away slowly as my wife sat in the car, fervently praying for my safety. Yet, for every frightening encounter, there were dozens of exhilarating ones. In one home, my wife spent time baking bread with a family of five children. Years later, we reunited with them at a camp meeting and were overjoyed to learn that the entire family of seven had been baptized.

I was soon called to serve in Grand Rapids, Michigan, but I hesitated to accept the appointment. I explained to Elder Nathaniel C. Wilson (grandfather of future General Conference President Ted Wilson) that I was currently studying with nineteen people. No other pastor was present to guide them toward baptism and church membership.

He looked at me and said firmly, "There comes a time when a man has to break loose."

In the end, I followed orders and moved to Grand Rapids. However, during the course of my ministry there, I realized that I needed to further my education. My classmate Walter Douglas, then a student at McGill University, encouraged me to apply to the same prestigious institution. I followed his advice, submitted my application, and was accepted.

Chapter 9

A Series of Divine Appointments

We set out for Montreal, Quebec, with high hopes but heavy hearts. While I had been accepted into the PhD program at McGill University, we had no place to live, and my wife had no job. As we drove into the city, the sheer density of Montreal's traffic—so different from the wide roads of Michigan—nearly overwhelmed me.

We stayed with a church member for a few days as we began our search, but the downtown core was discouraging. One afternoon, feeling particularly lost, I stopped the car on Beaver Hill Road. A gentleman tapped on my window and asked if we were lost. I told him we were looking for an accounting position for my wife.

"I know many of the officers in the IBM building," he said, pointing across Dorchester Avenue. "Go to the 8th floor; there is a gentleman there who can help."

We rushed over to the IBM building, but the meeting was a disappointment. The manager told us bluntly that nothing was available. Discouraged, we stepped into the elevator to leave. As the doors began to close, I spotted a sign through the glass for "Drake Personnel." On a whim, I told my wife, "We need to get out here."

At the Drake office, the atmosphere was entirely different. My wife took a proficiency test and passed with flying colors. Within minutes, she was told about a vacancy in a major accounting office. She met the manager and was hired on the spot. When my wife mentioned she didn't have a Canadian work permit yet, the manager simply smiled. "I can fix that. Go back to Michigan, pack your things, and the papers will be waiting in your mail."

With the job secured, we still needed a home. I drove to the McGill campus to meet my professor, but parking was impossible. After circling the block, I finally found a spot—and noticed a car with Michigan plates parked right next to me. I recognized it immediately as belonging to my friend Walter. I tucked a note under his wiper: "Here is Herbert. Please do not leave until I see you!"

When I returned from my meeting, Walter was waiting. Within twenty minutes of hearing our plight, he had spoken to the warden of the Anglican College. A student had just canceled their housing, and an apartment on the third floor was ours for $55 a month, utilities included.

Then we faced the final hurdle of moving our belongings. Harold, a kind church member in Michigan, offered us a solution: "I just bought a new truck. I'll drive you there myself."

We arrived at the Montreal Diocesan Theological College early on a Sunday morning. I was nervous about disrupting the Sunday worshipers, but as we pulled into the parking lot, a young couple—a nurse and her husband—stepped out to help us. Within an hour, all our belongings were moved in. When they noticed we had no mattress, the nurse didn't hesitate: "We have an extra one you can have."

Once again, when we reached the end of our own strength, the Spirit of Christ moved through others to provide exactly what we needed.

Bible Study Connections

Living in the student housing of the Anglican College was an unexpected blessing. Thirteen young pastors-in-training shared the building, and they formed a close-knit community. The spokesman for the group was Peter Blunt, a trained pharmacist who was studying for the ministry. His wife was the niece of the Anglican Bishop of Montreal.

One evening, Peter knocked on our door. "We are studying the Book of Ephesians," he said. "Would you be willing to join us?" I told him it would be a real pleasure. That evening of study was the beginning of a deep mutual respect between us.

The following week, I invited the group to our apartment. As we settled in, one of the students asked the question I knew was coming: "Why do you keep the Sabbath?"

I welcomed the opportunity to share our convictions. I explained that we believe that the Ten Commandments, the moral law given in Exodus 20, remain our guide. I pointed to the fourth commandment, where God specifically set aside the seventh day as holy. I spoke about the "sacred moments" of the Sabbath and how, by keeping it, we participate in the blessing and consecration God placed upon that day at Creation.

One student remarked, "It must be difficult for you to uphold that practice in today's world."

When it came time to close our session, Peter Blunt asked us all to kneel. I will never forget his first prayer request: he asked the Lord to reveal to him the true meaning and truth of the Sabbath.

Years later, after I had received my degree and we had departed from McGill, Peter became the pastor of three large Anglican churches on the South Shore of Montreal. When his fellow Anglican clergymen expressed concern about Seventh-day Adventists moving into their districts, Peter defended us.

"Two of them lived in our student housing," he told them. "They are fine Christian people. You should allow them to distribute their literature; there is no reason to be concerned about their activities." Through that simple friendship in a student apartment, a seed of understanding was planted that bore fruit long after we were gone.

The Dissertation

With my coursework and comprehensive exams behind me, I faced the final mountain: the dissertation. My topic was "A Critical Examination of Recent Theories about Eucharistic Origins." Because the specific literature I needed was not fully available at McGill, my wife and I set out for the Joseph Regenstein Library at the University of Chicago.

For two weeks, we stayed in Berrien Springs, commuting to Chicago every day. It was a massive enterprise; I spent hours scouring the stacks for rare research while my wife tirelessly copied every article I selected. We returned to Montreal carrying a huge box of data—the raw material for my life's work.

By this time, we had moved to St. Lambert on Montreal's South Shore. I had to sort the mountain of copies succinctly and begin the daunting task of writing. It was a difficult start, and I felt the weight of the work even more because my advisor, Dr. Kirby, was in France for a year teaching an extension course. I was writing entirely in a vacuum.

Upon his return, Dr. Kirby called me, concerned. "Herb, I haven't received a single page from you. What is the matter?"

"Dr. Kirby," I replied, "I have finished the entire work."

Stunned and excited, he demanded to see it. I rushed home, crossed back over the St. Lawrence River, and handed him my manuscript. I felt a pang of nerves as I apologized, "I am sorry, Dr. Kirby, but it is only handwritten."

"It doesn't matter," he said. "Leave it with me for two weeks."

To my surprise, he called me only two days later. He suggested that I move two items in the Table of Contents and noted that I had forgotten to list one reference in the bibliography. Then, he folded the document and handed it back. "Get it printed as fast as possible," he said. Aside from those two formal adjustments, there was not a single mistake in the entire work of 400 pages.

Thanks to my wife's reputation as a highly valued accountant at Alcan

Fiduciaries Limited, the company granted me an incredible privilege. I was given a 24-hour pass to the Alcan offices and assigned a private executive office on the 30th floor. There, suspended above the clouds with a panoramic view of downtown Montreal, I finalized my dissertation.

On the day of the oral examination. I stood before a panel of professors, including Father Bédard from Loyola College. When he posed the first question and I answered it with ease, I felt the tension break; in that moment, I knew the battle was won. As the examination drew to a close, a professor followed custom by picking up a glass to pour wine for a celebratory toast. Dr. Kirby intervened with a knowing smile: "He will not drink this," he said, honoring my convictions.

After the examination officially closed, Professor Bédard pulled me aside. "I like your German thoroughness and your objectivity," he said. With those words, the years of struggle, the cold nights on buses, and the long hours of research were validated. I was finally free to go home and share the news with my wife.

Moving Out West

In 1977, two years after receiving my doctorate from McGill, I received an invitation to move west to Alberta, Canada. I was asked to serve as the Chairman of the Bible Department at Canadian Union College (now Burman University).

We spent four years living in that beautiful, rugged landscape. While I thoroughly enjoyed the responsibility of leadership and the opportunity to shape the minds of future ministers, the role was not without its challenges. Before I left Montreal, someone had warned me that the college was a "real mission field," and upon my arrival, I quickly realized the truth of that statement. The needs of the department and the student body were vast, requiring a different kind of endurance than my academic studies had demanded.

*Blessed is every one that feareth the Lord;
that walketh in His ways.*

*For thou shalt eat the labour of thine
hands: happy shalt thou be, and it shall
be well with thee.*

*Thy wife shall be as a fruitful vine by the
sides of thine house: thy children like olive
plants round about thy table.*

*Behold, that thus shall the man be blessed
that feareth the Lord.*

*The Lord shall bless thee out of Zion:
and thou shalt see the good of Jerusalem
all the days of thy life.*

*Yea, thou shalt see thy children's children,
and peace upon Israel.*

—Psalm 128

Chapter 10

A Precious Baby Girl

My wife and I have never had a dull moment. Alongside our ministry, we shared a passion for teaching art. Then, during my first year teaching Bible courses at Canadian Union College (now Burman University), we received a surprising telephone call from friend, Pastor Gilbert Anderson, who was the president of the Maritime SDA Conference. He delivered a stunning message: "We have a newborn baby girl who deserves loving parents." We reacted instantly to the news. The very next day, my wife flew to Moncton, New

Brunswick, and with great joy received that beautiful baby into her arms. She brought the baby to our home in Lacombe, Alberta, and we named her Heidi Michelle. Heidi grew into a bright, talented young lady and became the proud mother of three handsome, intelligent sons: Tristan, Daniel, and Jason. As they pursue their education and move forward in life, our prayers and blessings remain with them always.

Chapter 11

A Call to Washington, D.C.

My next calling took us from the prairies of Lacombe to the bustling capital of the United States. I was appointed as an Associate Director of the Biblical Research Institute (BRI) for the General Conference of Seventh-day Adventists.

The transition was not without its practical burdens. We struggled to sell our newly built home in Alberta, and upon arriving in Washington, D.C., we found a housing market filled almost exclusively with older homes. Settling into the city took considerable time and patience.

In this new role, I found myself in a position of global influence. One of my most challenging and rewarding duties was organizing major Bible conferences across the Southern Asia Division and throughout Europe. These assignments required us to visit the major headquarters of the denomination worldwide.

It was a powerful and humbling experience. I was no longer just a student or a local teacher; I was now tasked with helping to steer the theological conversation for the entire world church, ensuring that our message remained clear and biblically sound across every continent.

Chapter 12

Mission to Southern Asia

My primary assignment at the Biblical Research Institute was to organize a series of high-level conferences for teachers and pastors throughout the Southern Asia Division. The central theme of our mission was the "Prophetic Messages of the Adventist Church," a topic that sits at the very heart of our denominational identity.

The logistics were formidable. One of my responsibilities was to select the teaching personnel from Andrews University and the Biblical Research Institute. With scholars departing from various locations, making punctual arrangements for the entire group was crucial. One missed connection could derail a conference that hundreds of pastors had traveled days to attend.

I saw clearly that God was at work, preparing the way for us to be received with openness and enthusiasm. Our itinerary was vast, spanning the distance from Singapore to Burma (Myanmar) and touching every country in between that fell within the division's territory.

Working in each of these diverse areas required a sensitive touch. We weren't just delivering lectures; we were engaging with local leaders to strengthen the biblical foundations of the church in some of the world's most challenging mission fields. Despite the complexity of the travel and the weight of the theological task, the Lord smoothed the path, ensuring that the message of the prophecies reached those who were called to share it.

Israel: Walking Where the Word Was Written

Of all the countries I had desired to see, Israel was the land of my dreams. Because of an unforeseen emergency in our travel schedule, we had to visit Israel first. Having spent a lifetime studying the Old Testament, I arrived with a deep foundation in the history of Judaism and the roots of Christianity.

In Jerusalem, we stayed at a center owned by our denomination. The building itself was a piece of history, having been constructed by the Turks about 500 years previously. Originally dedicated to Palestinian Christians, it had been abandoned during the war before the Adventist Church acquired it to serve as a haven for those visiting the Holy Land.

Walking through the city, I was struck by the tangible evidence of biblical history. At the Israel Museum, I saw one of the most remarkable archaeological finds of our time: the ossuary, or bone box, of Joseph Caiaphas. Chiseled out of sandstone and dating back 2,000 years, the box bore the inscriptions "Yosef bar Qayafa" and "Yosef bar Qafa." Seeing the name of the very high priest who had presided over the trial of Jesus brought the Gospel accounts into vivid reality.

We walked the Via Dolorosa—the Way of Suffering—tracing the path tradition says Jesus took from the residence of the high priest to the site of the crucifixion. We also made excursions to Bethlehem. While at the Church of the Nativity, they pointed out a small cave where Queen Helena, mother of Constantine the Great, believed Jesus was born. My designer's eye and historical intuition found this somewhat unreasonable—other nearby locations seemed better suited for a stable and birthplace, reminding me that tradition and archaeological fact are not always the same.

My mind was constantly occupied with the religious landscape of the first century. I thought of the three main groups that shaped the Jerusalem Jesus knew:

- The Pharisees, who sat in "Moses' seat" and were meticulously devoted to the Mosaic Law.

- The Sadducees, who held the power of the priesthood but did not believe in the resurrection—a position some modern rabbis still ponder today.

- The Essenes, a conservative group that likely fled the perceived corruption of the Jerusalem priesthood.

The Essenes relocated to the desert, settling near the fortress of Masada and the cliffs of Qumran. In 1946, the world was changed when 900 of their documents were discovered in ceramic jars within those caves. It was fascinating to picture them in their scriptorium, carefully copying the sacred texts that are now displayed for the world to see in Jerusalem. Standing there, I felt a deep connection to those ancient scribes; like them, I had spent my life trying to preserve and understand the Word of God.

Indonesia: From the Exhaust of Jakarta to the Jungles of Manado

Our first landing in Indonesia was in Jakarta. I must admit, the city did not excite me. At that time, there was no exhaust control on the vehicles, and the fumes from the buses and cars were so overpowering that we had to wear masks just to breathe. It was a relief when that short visit ended and we departed for the western reaches of Indonesia.

The Jungle Church

Upon arriving in Manado, we were greeted by a mid-sized, incredibly friendly congregation. While our team presented the main lectures, I was asked to travel to a different church for the Sabbath service. Early that morning, a young preacher traveled a great distance to pick me up and lead me into the heart of the jungle.

There, in a clearing hacked out of the dense tropical greenery, stood a very respectable church. It was my privilege to speak to a remarkably attentive group of believers. This church community had been established by Pastor Detamore, a dedicated American evangelist who had been one of my teachers at Emmanuel Missionary College. This man, who a deep love for Christ, had ventured into this predominantly Muslim area. Through his tireless ministry, many had been moved to accept the Adventist message, creating a vibrant foundation for the work I was now continuing.

After the service, I was invited to a local home for lunch, followed by community visits. One young man approached me with a humble request: "Would you come with me and pray for my uncle? He is a Muslim." I went with him, and we were received with great kindness. As I left his uncle's home, I noticed beautiful, tall irises growing in the front gardens—a splash of delicate color against the wild jungle backdrop.

A Divine Intervention

While there, we learned the harrowing history of the church's construction. In the early days, some members of the community did not tolerate a Christian presence and decided to burn the building to the ground.

One night, a group of men armed with torches approached the church. Just as they reached the perimeter, something extraordinary happened: every light inside and outside the building suddenly flashed on, illuminating the entire clearing. Terrified, the men believed God must be intervening in a way they could not comprehend. They immediately fled, and no one ever attempted to harm the church building again. To me, this was extraordinary evidence that God is alive and watches over the places dedicated to His holy name.

Final Farewells

An American mission pilot offered to fly us across the water to visit an indigenous tribe that had accepted Christianity recently. It was a tempting three-hour flight, but our rigid schedule unfortunately did not allow for the detour.

Before we left Manado, we held a final service. A male choir performed the hymn, “Alas! and Did My Savior Bleed?” They sang the line, "For such a wretch as I," with such deep, soul-searching conviction that it left a permanent mark on my heart.

Before we boarded our flight to the Philippines, the mission pilot took us on a short aerial tour. From the plane, the Manado jungle looked like a vast, green carpet stretching to the horizon. As we landed at the local airport to say our final goodbyes, it dawned on me what a joy it was to encounter so many different languages, complexions, and cultures. I had gained a wealth of insight into the human family.

The Philippines: Faith on Stilts

George Reid and I arrived in the Philippines just before the weekend, allowing me to experience my very first Philippine Sabbath service. While I had known Filipino students during my college years who had shared their history with me—particularly the complex legacy of 400 years of Spanish rule—nothing compared to seeing the life of the church firsthand.

Our primary mission was to present a series of lectures on biblical prophecy at the Adventist seminary. During our travels, we were accompanied by a young local seminary graduate. When we asked about his ministry, he told us he was responsible for sixteen different churches.

"How do you possibly reach them all?" I asked, stunned by the workload.

"I only have a bicycle," he explained simply. "And many times, I have to carry it across streams to reach the congregations."

I witnessed the humble conditions under which many of the people lived—traditional houses built on stilts, with open space underneath for storage. I noticed many rats nearby and asked how they coped with the pests. He laughed softly and said, "We just leave them alone; they don't bother us." It was a testament to the local resilience and their ability to focus on what truly mattered despite their environment.

As we traveled through the countryside, I was struck by the manual labor involved in church construction. I saw no motorized cranes or heavy machinery. Instead, workmen were digging foundations for a new church school using nothing but spades and shovels. It was backbreaking, dirty work, and it was clear that funds for modern equipment simply did not exist.

Yet, despite the poverty and the primitive tools, a striking sight emerged as we drove: in almost every community, there stood a stately, majestic church building. They were impeccably maintained and stood as silent witnesses to the sacrifice of the people. They may have lacked machinery, but they clearly lacked nothing in devotion.

With our lectures completed and our hearts moved by the dedication of the Filipino brothers and sisters, we prepared for our next destination: Pakistan.

Pakistan: Miracles in the Dust of Lahore

Our arrival in Lahore was marked by sweltering heat. We were met at the airport by Pastor Johnson in a minibus that, quite frankly, smelled like a livestock carrier. With a smile, he explained that a generous donor in America had sent him a brand-new van, but realizing his members paid their tithes in livestock, he had sold the new vehicle to buy this sturdy "animal transporter" instead. It was a practical solution for a humble field.

The Adventist school where we stayed was surrounded by formidable high walls and a heavy steel gate. This security was a somber necessity due to the historical tensions between religious groups in the region. However, those very walls later became a symbol of grace.

Years after our visit, I learned that during a period of violent unrest, a mob had planned to break into the school. They were stopped by an elderly Pakistani man who reminded them of the Adventists' kindness. "During the war," he told them, "these people opened their gates to protect us. Do not ever dare harm them." Because the Adventists shared the local community's respect for a diet free of pork and alcohol, a bond of deep, mutual respect had been forged that saved lives.

Lessons from the Village

We traveled to a small village where time seemed to have stood still. We saw water buffaloes circling large stones to grind grain and residents gathering buffalo droppings to dry as "pancakes" for cooking fuel, as wood was a luxury few could afford.

Despite the scarcity, their homes were models of neatness and hospitality. Inside, we often found a single brass plate on the wall and a small table with a floral arrangement—simple touches that turned a humble dwelling into a sanctuary. We observed people who were in a time of mourning, which lasted a full week, noting the great seriousness and dignity they afforded to the loss of a loved one.

The Insect and the Heart

Our meetings were held in a church built entirely of concrete—the only material available. Before we departed, a local contractor prepared a magnificent meal for us to eat. My "German thoroughness" couldn't help but notice the lack of porcelain dishes; instead, they used recycled tin cans. I also noticed a swarm of flies hovering over the food preparation area.

I whispered my concern to my Swiss colleague, Brother Yaki, who shared a startling story from his own experience. He had once been served a drink into which a large insect had fallen. As he reached to remove it, he was quickly cautioned: "If you do that, you will offend your hosts and break the ties we have worked so hard to build." He just swallowed it down, choosing the relationship over his own comfort. This story reinforced a vital truth for our mission: sympathy, kindness, and love are far more important than pointing out differences.

Throughout my journey—from the schoolrooms of Germany to the jungles of

Manado and the dust of Pakistan—I have learned that every person is a human being desiring friendship and interaction. When you show people that you truly care for them, the barriers of complexion, language, and religion fall away. Love is the only language that is understood everywhere.

India: From the Golden Temple to the Streets of Calcutta

Our transition from Pakistan into India began under the shade of massive mango trees, where luggage carriers waited to help us across the border. Pastor Johnson, our blonde American colleague from Minnesota, greeted the Punjabi border guards with hearty hugs—a beautiful illustration of the bridge-building power of the mission. We stepped across the line and entered the land of the Sikhs.

The Golden Temple and Cultural Lessons

In Amritsar, we visited the Golden Temple. Following tradition, we removed our shoes and walked barefoot through a basin of water. The heat that day was staggering; I stepped onto the solid tile for only a second before the searing temperature forced me back into the shadows.

Inside, I encountered two Sikh priests, seated with immense dignity in white robes and long white beards. In my enthusiasm, I raised my camera to capture the scene, but a hand from behind me immediately pushed my arm down. It was a sharp lesson: to visit a culture is to respect its sanctity. I realized that a missionary must not only study theology but also the philosophy and "soul" of the people they serve.

Spicer Memorial College: A Fragrant Welcome

We traveled to Spicer Memorial College in Pune, where the college president, Dr. Cherian, welcomed us with incredible warmth. Our entire team was called onto the auditorium stage, and each of us was draped with a garland of fragrant Indian blossoms.

My living quarters provided another cross-cultural adjustment. I shared an apartment with my colleague, Dr. Shea, a former surgeon. When I discovered a shrew, a mouse-like creature, scurrying across my bedroom floor, Dr. Shea—who had served in Trinidad—was unfazed. “Herb, don't worry about them,” he said. “I'm used to these creatures. Take my room.”

At the college, the poverty of the students was visible even in their devotion. I noticed that many young women could not attend Sabbath services every week because two girls often shared a single “Sabbath dress.” They had to take turns, one attending one week and the other the next.

Encounters with Leadership and Legacy

Dr. Cherian arranged for me to meet the president of the University of Pune, a prestigious institution where Winston Churchill had once operated during World War II. We passed through a gauntlet of six guards in classy turbans and traditional uniforms. The president was a man of few words but enormous gravity; I felt I was in the presence of someone who influenced the very heart of the Indian government.

Later, an Anglo-Indian friend and former Spitfire pilot took me to the Mahatma Gandhi Museum. He shared a story that has haunted me ever since. When Gandhi was asked why he never became a Christian, he replied, "I have never met one." He had experienced such mistreatment from "Christian" British authorities—being kicked off trains and treated as a second-class citizen—that he never saw the love of Christ reflected in the people who claimed His name. Yet he led his nation to independence through the very principles of non-retaliation he found in the Sermon on the Mount.

The Monsoon and the Sidewalks of Calcutta

As the monsoon season arrived, the rains brought beauty but also bacteria. I became severely ill with a high fever. When I asked for an aspirin, I was shocked to find there was only one available on the entire campus. This scarcity of basic medicine was a stark reminder of the "mission field" we were in.

Our journey concluded in Calcutta. I was heartbroken by the sight of the wide sidewalks covered with men and families who lived and died there. I learned the tragic reason: many were there because they could not afford the dowries for their daughters and had been forced to sell everything they owned.

The trip ended as it began—with a deep appreciation for the peacemakers like Gandhi and a renewed determination to be a "real Christian" to those who have never met one.

Burma: Faith Amid the Shadows of Rangoon

Our next assignment was Burma. At that time, it was a strictly socialist country, where the appearance of Buddhist piety masked a rigid and often dangerous political environment. Our visit was a study in caution and divine protection.

The Secret Sanctuary

The Seventh-day Adventist church in Rangoon was located, quite precariously, right next to a military base. To ensure the authorities did not see us, the conference president met us in a tiny French-made truck. He drove directly into a hidden hallway under the church's overhang. Only once we were safely inside, away from the eyes of the nearby soldiers, were we able to step out and enter the sanctuary.

Despite the restriction that forbade us from public speaking, even in our own churches, the local leaders were resourceful. They would shuttle Dr. Shea, Dr. Cherian, and me back and forth from our government-supervised hotel in a minibus. Under the Lord's protection, I was able to preach several times to a people hungry for the Word.

The Upper Room

One of the most moving experiences was when a church member, an Indian engineer, invited us to his home to meet his wife, children, and mother-in-law. It was strictly illegal for foreigners to visit private residences or stay in civilian quarters.

Knowing the risks, he picked us up after dark and led us to his apartment. We spent the evening in an upstairs attic room—a modern "upper room"—sharing the promises of God and praying together. These lovely people were spiritually isolated, and those hours of fellowship were a rare treasure for all of us. As we slipped back into our hotel in the darkness, I felt a deep sense of gratitude for the "God who sees" even in the most restricted places.

Rangoon: A City of Contrasts

The city of Rangoon was a place of unexpected beauty and visible struggle. We walked through areas that felt almost romantic, with stylish Burmese architecture and delis reminiscent of Barclay's in London. Yet, in front of shops, I saw stacks of old, used American magazines being sold for a pittance—a small link to the outside world.

I was particularly moved by the stories of the youth. Education was difficult to obtain under the socialist regime; therefore, many young men risked everything to flee to India. They traveled a dangerous path through the wilderness, knowing that if the police caught them, they faced prison time. Meeting students at Spicer Memorial College who had successfully made that perilous journey was a testament to their incredible hunger for a Christian education.

A Final Blessing

As we prepared to leave, the atmosphere of the country remained heavy. At the airport, we boarded a small, aging plane with loose seats, dodging massive cumulus clouds as we took off.

But it was a moment at the hotel checkout that stayed with me most. As I handed over my keys and paid the bill, the lady at the desk looked at me and said quietly, "God bless you." In a socialist country where such a phrase could be dangerous, her words were a bold testimony. I looked back at her and replied, "God bless you too."

It was a final reminder that no matter how high the walls or how strict the government, the citizens of God's kingdom will always find a way to recognize one another.

Burma to India

Our departure from Burma was as harrowing as our arrival. Dr. Shea and I boarded a small, vintage 1940s airplane with seats that rattled and shifted beneath us. As we crossed the Indian Ocean, the pilot performed a delicate dance, maneuvering the aging craft around towering cumulus clouds. After a long and weary flight, we touched down in Calcutta.

The Temple of Kali

Dr. Cherian met us upon our arrival, eager to show us the historical and religious heart of the city. We visited the temple devoted to the goddess Kali—the deity whose name gave Calcutta its own. The scene was overwhelming. Scores of women stood in long lines, seeking to pay for the blessing of fertility.

While we were there, a grim ritual was underway: the sacrifice of one hundred young goats. I watched, heart-heavy, as a priest raised a razor-sharp sword. With one swift, clinical sweep, the sacrifice was complete. When I asked what became of the animals, I was told they went into a communal food pool. To an observer of the living God, the sight of such slaughter was excruciating. I could not watch another moment of it; the pain and the darkness of the rite stayed with me long after we left the temple grounds.

The Sidewalks of Calcutta

The next morning, as a taxi carried us through the city, we witnessed the daily struggle for survival on a massive scale. On endless sidewalks stretching into the distance, hundreds upon hundreds of people lived in the open air. I watched one man stoop over a hole in the pavement filled with murky water; he scooped it up with both hands to wash his face—his morning ablution in the only "basin" he had.

The city was a graveyard of British grandeur. We drove past massive, stately buildings once erected by the Empire, now weathered under Indian authority. Beneath the bridges, the local poor had hung tarps down to the sidewalk to create "walls" for their families. As our bus idled in the heavy traffic, I watched the thick, black exhaust fumes billow directly behind those tarps where children were sleeping. It was a constant, suffocating exposure to poison.

Reflections on Grace

A colleague at Spicer Memorial College, an Australian doctor, had offered to take me deep into these poverty-stricken areas to conduct social studies. He promised to show me sights I wouldn't believe existed. However, the constraints of my schedule and my upcoming appointments in New Delhi meant I had to decline.

As we prepared to depart from India, my heart filled with new gratitude. Seeing the "least of these" in such desperate conditions made me realize how often we fail to appreciate the basic blessings of food, clothing, and safe housing. We live in a world of abundance, yet so many live in the shadow of lack.

With these sobering lessons etched in our minds, we turned our eyes toward our next destination and a very different world: China.

China:
Books, Buffaloes, and the Red Army

Our final series of meetings in Asia was scheduled to take place at the Hong Kong Seventh-day Adventist Hospital, an institution established by Dr. Harry Miller. These sessions, spanning several days, were attended by church leaders, pastors, and a small group of others. It was a truly delightful setting for our gathering. At that time, the hospital was administered directly from the United States.

Once the meetings had concluded, we were able to explore the city and attend services at several local Seventh-day Adventist churches. If you were to visit Hong

Kong today, you would find it unrecognizable compared to that era. Now controlled by the full authority of the Chinese government—which oversees all modern renovations—the city has transformed significantly. During our stay, church officials were kind enough to arrange a visit for us to mainland China.

Several of us were carrying books intended for a pastor from northern China. We boarded a train from Hong Kong and traveled toward the border to deliver these volumes, which we had brought all the way from America. They were primarily theological and historical texts the pastor had specifically requested, and several of them were quite heavy.

Upon our arrival, we searched for the pastor, but he was nowhere to be found. A sense of unease began to set in as we wondered what to do with the books here in mainland China. As I looked across the wooden walkway directly into the offices of the Red Army, the reality of the situation hit me: I was standing inside Communist China, carrying American books written in English, with no contact person in sight. I stood there, weighing my options and wondering what our next move should be.

A friend suggested that we simply distribute the books to the people passing by. Taking a leap of faith, I reached into my luggage, pulled out the volumes, and began handing them to the passersby. I truly believe God protected us in that moment; although the soldiers saw exactly what we were doing, not one of them approached us or questioned our actions.

Leaving the border of southern China behind, we followed the arrangements made by the Hong Kong conference leaders for our visit further north. A minibus was waiting for us on the other side. Our group boarded the vehicle, and we drove away into the interior of the country.

We were driven further north by a young man who spoke not a word of English, hired through a company in Hong Kong. Our tour guide, however, was quite the opposite; he encouraged us to speak openly and freely. He even shared the story of his recent conversion to Christianity. His English was remarkably polished—a skill he attributed to his constant work with tourists. Before we parted, he asked for a favor: a written recommendation to help bridge the gap with a boss who didn't favor him. Upon my return to Washington, I followed through and sent his employer a glowing review.

I vividly recall our first stop: a man was leading a flock of about twenty ducks along the roadside. The ground was sodden, and heavy trucks thundered past, spraying the "shepherd" and his ducks with plumes of mud.

We asked our guide if he could take us to a village where we could truly experience Chinese culture. "Certainly, I can do that. It's no problem," he replied, eventually pulling the minibus over. Some of us were wearing light coats as we stepped out to visit a small community nearby.

The first thing that caught my eye was a weathered red building that looked as though it were on the verge of collapsing. When I inquired about its significance, I was surprised to learn it was the local dental office. Nearby, a woman stood with her baby; I asked if I could take a photo, but she declined, so I moved on.

In the distance, I spotted what appeared to be a marketplace. The ground was thick with mud from a recent rain. A large group of people had gathered in a circle, but as soon as they saw us in our white coats, they began to retreat toward their homes, clearly hesitant to be seen. Our guide quickly intervened, reassuring them that we had come as friends.

Once they felt at ease, the villagers returned to the circle, welcoming us warmly. One memory stands out vividly: I took a photo of a five-year-old boy standing next to a hog. The animal was so large it stood as tall as the boy himself. I still have that photograph in my collection today.

As we made our way back from the marketplace, I passed the woman and baby I had encountered earlier. This time, she stepped forward and invited me to take a photo of her and her son. Nearby, a water buffalo stood quietly in a small pond, completing the serene scene.

By then, our group had worked up quite an appetite, so we stopped at a local restaurant. The architecture was striking; though aged, you could tell it had been built in a romantic style, surrounded by a peaceful pond and structures that must have been magnificent in their prime.

Once inside, we were treated to an incredible feast of thirteen courses. The hospitality was relentless—as soon as a plate was empty, the kitchen staff reappeared to refill it with more of the dishes we had enjoyed. They were constantly attentive, ensuring our glasses were never empty of drinks or mineral water. Just as we thought we couldn't eat another bite, the waitress arrived with yet another massive tray of food. It was a supper I will never forget!

Eventually, we headed to our accommodations for the night. The following morning, we visited a center where foreigners were invited to shop for local Chinese goods. Near a Buddhist temple just outside the area, I met a young Chinese boy. Beside the temple stood a long staircase leading to the top of the building, offering a panoramic view of the entire city.

As we climbed the stairs together, the boy looked at me and said, "Sir, I don't want any money. All I want is to practice speaking English with you."

"That's perfectly fine," I replied.

He was incredibly friendly and eager to help. He offered to accompany me to the store to assist with my shopping or help me exchange currency. With his help, I picked out several items for my wife and a few small gifts for my daughter.

Later, I noticed that the local burial customs were quite different from those we are used to in the West. As we drove past a high mountain, I saw numerous wide openings carved into the rock face. Intrigued, I asked someone about their purpose.

"Those are the burial places for the deceased," he explained. What a remarkable sight—entire histories etched into the side of the mountain!

As we traveled throughout the country, we encountered a world that was both vastly different and deeply challenging. Yet the Chinese people were remarkably kind and accommodating; we never encountered any hostility as Westerners.

Eventually, it was time to leave China and return home to the United States. While there are countless other stories I could tell, these few experiences remain the most unforgettable in my mind.

The journey left me with a profound sense of gratitude. I am deeply thankful to be an American and to enjoy the freedoms I have known throughout my life. My one sincere hope is that we, as Americans, truly treasure our liberty. We must never take it for granted, for once our freedom is lost, we would be truly adrift.

Our travels were far from over, as many other regions—including the major cities of Europe—remained to be visited. Nevertheless, I am deeply thankful for the experiences we gathered throughout the

Southern Asia Division. I truly hope and trust that the efforts we planted there will one day bear much fruit.

Reflecting on the time spent with the people there often leaves my heart heavy. It was difficult being unable to provide the financial assistance they so clearly needed. However, we offered them something else: we shared our common hope in the return of our Savior. With our work in Southern Asia concluded, we turned our focus toward our next destination, preparing to visit and support our people in Kyiv, Ukraine, and Moldova.

Kyiv: Angels in the Concrete

Kyiv, the majestic capital city of Ukraine, is a city of striking contrasts. I marveled at its historic, regal architecture, yet these beautiful landmarks were often overshadowed by the massive, crumbling concrete structures left behind by the socialist era.

Dr. Shea and I were greeted with the profound warmth that characterizes our Ukrainian brethren. At lunch early in our visit, we met Dr. Scharfenberg, who had been sent to evaluate nutritional programs across Asia. We soon moved to a supersized hall for the Sabbath services. The crowd was so vast I couldn't even estimate the numbers, but the energy of their worship was dynamic.

A Providential Translation

One major concern for our presentation was finding a translator, but the Lord had already orchestrated a solution. My translator was a young woman with an incredible story. She and her twin sister had fled a difficult life in Siberia to escape an alcoholic father. During their long journey by train, they met an elderly Adventist man who shared the Gospel with them. By the time they reached Kyiv, they were baptized and ready to serve.

Remarkably, that very Sabbath night—only hours after translating for us—both sisters boarded a flight to Montreal. They had both been granted all-expenses-paid scholarships to Canadian Union College, our college in Alberta, Canada. Seeing the Lord guide these young women step by step, from the depths of Siberia to the classrooms of Canada, was a powerful testimony to His global watch care.

Seventeen Years of Faithfulness

Following the service, Dr. Scharfenberg and I were invited for lunch by a kind couple. As soon as we entered their apartment, the atmosphere told me this was a home dedicated to God. We were joined by a tall high school student named Pavel, who served as our translator. It was through him that we met a sister in the faith whose story I will never forget.

She had once held a prestigious position in a chemical company with a home and a comfortable salary. When her boss demanded she work on the Sabbath, she refused. The consequences were bitter and swift: her salary was slashed, she was moved to a cold, unfriendly room, and she was assigned to sweep the city sidewalks.

"This lasted for seventeen years," she told me quietly. She reached out her hands—hardened and calloused from nearly two decades of manual labor—not to complain, but to take a stringed instrument from the wall. She then began to sing, and her voice was like the voice of an angel.

Her sacrifice touched me deeply. I, too, had faced life-threatening events and hardship, but her quiet endurance in the face of systemic oppression was a different kind of bravery. Before we left, we joined in earnest prayer. We knew we were leaving them in a place of great difficulty, but we also knew they were not alone.

An Intercessory Prayer

Today, as we look at the tragic conflict between Russia and Ukraine, my wife and

I frequently lift our hearts on behalf of our people in those war-torn territories. The calloused hands of that singer and the courage of those sisters remain in our memories, fueling our prayers for their safety and the soon return of the Prince of Peace.

A Global Brotherhood in Christ

In retrospect, I look back on those assignments with a deep sense of gravity. We were tasked with delivering essential truths within a very short time span to people of vastly different races, languages, and national histories. From the bustling streets of India to the quiet, watchful apartments of Kyiv, the pressure was immense.

And yet, a beautiful phenomenon occurred in every country we visited: we felt at home.

Despite the cultural chasms and the political borders that stood between us, we were never truly strangers. We found that we were united at the heart because of our Lord Jesus Christ. Whether we were sharing a meal of boiled potatoes in a village or standing before a crowded hall in Ukraine, the Spirit of God created a familiar bond that transcended our differences.

The Final Hope

It is my humble prayer that our efforts, though they seem small in the face of such global need, will bear much fruit in the years to come. The "seeds" of justification by faith—the assurance that we are saved by His grace—were planted in fertile soil.

My greatest hope is to see the faces of those believers again—the students in the Philippines, the families in the "upper rooms" of Burma, and the faithful souls in the Southern Asia Division. I look forward to that day when there will be no more borders, no more poverty, and no more "exhaust fumes," as we meet together in the kingdom of God.

Pictures

August Kiesler, Herbert's father

Martha Kiesler, Herbert's mother

Herbert Kiesler as a child

Herbert Kiesler, 1959

August 13, 1961

Wedding of Minodora Grigorean and Herbert Kiesler at the Seventh-day Adventist Church in Neunkirchen, Saar, Germany

Pastor Kiesler's ordination to the ministry by Elder Nathaniel Wilson, 1967

Dr. and Mrs. Kiesler with Heidi Kiesler

While serving as chair of the theology department at Canadian Union College in Alberta, Canada, 1980

With Miroslav Kis at Canadian Union College, Lacombe, Alberta, 1981

At Spicer Memorial College, Southern Asia Division Bible Conference, 1983

Dr. Kiesler with his team and other ministers

Dr. Kiesler with his Biblical Research Institute team at the General Conference of Seventh-day Adventists

Dr. Kiesler preaching

September 1998, Butchart Gardens, Vancouver Island

Class of 1957 reunion, Marienhöhe seminary, Darmstadt, Germany

Dr. and Mrs. Kiesler

Dr. and Mrs. Kiesler at Berrien Springs, Michigan, 2021

Dr. Kiesler's grandsons:
Daniel Alexander and Tristan Alexander